THESE ARE THE DAYS

Written by Alastair Machray MBE
and a legion of rabid Reds.

Design: Colin Sumpter
Production: Michael McGuinness
Published by the Liverpool Echo/Reach Plc
Marketing and Communications: Rachel
Cunningham and Claire Brown.

The authors and publishers are grateful to
the following individuals for their time and
help in providing material for this book:
Paul Gorst, Dr Gillian Cook, Maria Breslin,
Colin Lane, The Press Association.

First Edition
Published in Great Britain in 2020.
Published and produced by the
Liverpool Echo/Reach Plc.
5 St Paul's Square, Third Floor, Liverpool, L3 9SJ

All Rights Reserved. No part of this publication
may be reproduced, stored in a retrieval system,
or transmitted in any form, or by any means,
electronic, mechanical, photocopying, recording
or otherwise without the prior permission in
writing of the copyright holders, nor be otherwise
circulated in any form of binding of cover other
than in which it is published and without a similar
condition being imposed on the subsequent
publisher.

In instances where Reach PLC may not own the
copyright, every effort has been made to trace
the original copyright holder. Any oversight will be
rectified in future editions of this publication.

ISBN: 9781911613954
Printed and bound by Buxton Press

Contents

Introduction by Alastair Machray MBE	4
Paul Gorst's Story of a Season	6
You'll Never Walk Alone	12
Madness	16
A Special Bond	30
Rituals	40
Lane's Lens	52
The Moment of Triumph	68
The People Who Matter	80
Why Red?	90
The Twelfth Man by Paul Gorst	104
Biographies	107

By ALASTAIR MACHRAY MBE.
Editor Liverpool Daily Post and Liverpool Echo 1995-2020

I once sat down for dinner with Brendan Rodgers when he was manager of Liverpool. As you can imagine in a city centre restaurant, we weren't left alone much with one diner after another coming over to shake Rodgers' hand and have a chat. They were even coming in off the street.

After a while I said I was sorry and that I was sure it wasn't like this when he was manager of Swansea. 'Well', he said, 'It was and it wasn't. The difference is that in Swansea people would come up to you and ask you who was in the team for Saturday. 'In Liverpool,' he said, 'they come up and tell you who SHOULD be in the team for Saturday,

I remember once going to my email inbox and the first email I opened was from someone who began: 'Dear editor - you won't print this letter cos you are Red shite......'

So with a sigh I closed it down and opened my next email. Not Dear Editor or anything. It simply began: 'Now listen here you tuppenny ha'penny blue-nosed bastard....'

So I get football in this city. Mostly. And I get football generally. I love it, hate it. Like a helpless smackhead I wish I could kick it but I can't.

I'm a Newcastle fan (ok, spare me the patronising shit) so I know what it's like to travel the length of the country in a transit van wishing you hadn't had that last pint, I know what it's like to be so nervous before a game that you can't eat. I know what it's like to be a crap husband and father simply because a game of football was lost.

I know what it's like to win a match, and to want to dress up smart, hit the bar and talk to everyone who'll listen. And then get so drunk you fall asleep on the couch and miss the Match of the Day.

I know all that.

But I don't know what it's like to win. I don't know what it's like to have that sense of glory-entitlement that every Reds fan seems to feel. I don't know what it's like to despise mediocrity. I don't know what it's like to care so deeply, to own with such jealousy, that greedy absentee owners are hounded out of town, their tail between their legs where once hung balls of steel.

And I wanted to know.

For me, Covid was the crystallizing agent. The control experiment where football fans were given a drug that heightened the nerves, the passion, the anxiety, just to see how they would respond. So mid-pandemic I asked Reds fans what it was all about? Just what was the deal? I opened a Pandora's Box.

I was taken on a journey deep into the heart, inside the soul and through the contorted pathways of the anxious mind. In the end I sought a guide, psychologist Dr Gillian Cook, to help me make sense of it all. A lecturer in Sport and Exercise Psychology and Sport and Performance Psychologist at Liverpool John Moores University, Gillian is the first team and club sport psychologist at Dundee United and has worked with organisations including British Swimming, British Athletics, Scottish Hockey, Loughborough Sport, Nike, the NHS,and BBC.

She helped me understand that Lockdown means that this title win, far from being tainted, was extra special. That it would live forever in the memory of fans everywhere - not just Reds.

I read through thousands of comments and observations from Reds fans right across the globe. One word kept coming up. 'Family.' Gill taught me how that sense of belonging was essential for humans to thrive and, in a pandemic, perhaps to survive.

She explained how You'll Never Walk Alone actually works. That it is really IS more than a song and that the fabled Anfield Twelfth Man was actually more than a cliché.

And the Klopp factor, Goodness. I laughed early in his Anfield reign when Joey Barton, never short of a tapdance when the spotlight's on him, described Klopp as 'The German cheerleader.' I realize now that whatever he brings, he and Liverpool FC are a match made in heaven.

And Gillian helped me understand a little more about the sentimentality that runs deep through the Red DNA.

We once carried a death notice in the Echo that read; *'To Vinnie. Don't worry mate, you've bounced back from worse than this.'* And my privileged visit to the private emotions of a legion of Reds fans convinced me that whoever placed that notice was probably right. You're never really dead on Merseyside - and when there is something special to celebrate they wake you up and make sure you're part of the party.

To Doctor Cook I say thanks for the brains and for loving footy unconditionally, like I do. To Maria Beslin, Paul Dove, Colin Sumpter and Rachel Cunnigham, thanks for refusing to accept less than excellent. To Paul Gorst, thanks for being an expert witness and to Ceri Gould - a bloody Rugby fan - thanks for the idea.

To every one of the hundreds of Reds fans who let me inside their heads, I say a humble thank you. Even to the total barmpots.

And if Karma brings me back a second time and the Reds win the League, I don't want to be a goat.

You'll Never Walk Alone.

PAUL GORST looks back at the season which made Liverpool champions of England for the 19th time

There's a sign that adorns Liverpool's walls, right at the heart of Anfield.

It is a saying from their manager, Jürgen Klopp. One that neatly encapsulates everything this iconic venue of sporting excellence represents. The phrase is essentially the reason it exists to this day.

"This is a place for big football moments," reads the succinct pearl of wisdom from Klopp.

As the manager who has just become the first in three decades to lead Liverpool to a domestic league title, he now knows that more than most.

From virtually the first whistle of the 2019-20 Premier League season, they were several cuts above.

Perhaps fueled by the agony of missing out on last year's title, the Reds hit their stride early and didn't look back once.

After a previous term left them without the Holy Grail - despite tasting defeat just once - it would have been easy to fall away, to let the bitter disappointment of silver lead to a regression.

After collecting 97 points - a tally that would have won them the crown in 25 other Premier League seasons - and still only ending up as runners-up, just how would this Liverpool team pick themselves up, dust themselves down and convince themselves that they could overthrow a domestically dominant Manchester City?

For Klopp, it was simple.

He told the ECHO exactly how in trademark style during a chat in the season's formative stages.

"How do we improve? You only have to look at your passport, as long as you are not dead, you can improve, that is how it is," was Klopp's trademark summary in his Melwood office last year.

For that, the Champions League victory in Madrid three weeks later must take ample credit for instilling what has since become an unshakable belief, into this Liverpool team.

Winning the biggest trophy in club football in the European Cup told this Reds squad, they had the minerals to pull up their boot straps and try again. Without major surgery in the transfer market, the famed 'mentality monsters' blitzed through the competition, running away with the league to wrap it up with a record seven games left to play.

But just how did Klopp's Liverpool summon the fortitude to go one better?

It started back in July 2019 when the Reds reconvened for pre-season at Melwood. The mood was a relaxed one across the summer months. Winning the European Cup will do that to you. No new signings were needed as Klopp took the decision to keep together the team that had come within a whisker of a Premier League and Champions League double the season previous.

The 2019 European Cup final eased any lingering concerns that this was a squad full of nearly-men. Lifting the biggest prize in club football in Madrid on June 1 convinced everyone connected to the club that they could be successful. As a result, Klopp's players were emboldened, firmly believing they could topple City this term.

Bringing the curtain up on the season, Liverpool ripped through a newly-promoted Norwich in the first half, eventually running out 4-1 winners.

It would be two-and-a-half months before a single point would be dropped as a rampant Reds ran up a six-point advantage after nine games.

With last year's gap between the clubs proving to be wafer-thin, such an advantage was a healthy one for Klopp's men. But they only had aspirations of increasing it as autumn turned to winter. Victories over Southampton, Arsenal, Chelsea, Newcastle, Burnley, Sheffield United and Leicester were all totted up as the Reds found a new gear early on.

A 17-game winning run may have been brought to a halt at Old Trafford on October 20, but something was stirring. It would take a further four months before another point was dropped by Klopp's men.

Decisive wins over the likes of Manchester City, Everton and Leicester City (on Boxing Day) were all racked up as the gap continued to widen.

Each City stumble was greeted heartily from the Reds faithful as Pep Guardiola's champions suffered damaging defeats against Norwich and Wolves and a draw with Spurs.

But as Liverpool's lead grew more substantial, a variety of players were keen to stick to the party line after each and every week. Regardless of how impressive the performance or how significant the result, the Liverpool squad, as per their manager's demands, were keeping their feet firmly on the ground.

Six points became nine with a 3-1 win over City at Anfield on November 11 before the squad flew out to their respective international camps with a spring in their step.

Unable to get a real chance to analyse the result and performance with his team, it wasn't until nearly two weeks later that Klopp and his players met to discuss that huge victory over their title rivals.

Liverpool met up to pick the bones of the game against City, as is customary, and the collective mood was understated. They knew they had taken a giant stride towards their goal, but there was much work still to be done.

Celebrations were minimal as the team gave themselves a quick pat on the back before readying themselves for what was promising to be a make-or-break December. The overriding message remained the same. Nothing was won yet.

Between November 23 and January 5, Liverpool would play 14 times. That included a trip to Qatar for what was a draining couple of games in a successful Club World Cup campaign. Taking their eye off the ball could easily have resulted in that nine-point advantage dissipating. "Nothing has changed, we just have to win football games and the rest is not interesting to us," said Klopp after a nervy win over Brighton at the end of November. "We don't go in the dressing room and look at other results and start celebrating. There is nothing to celebrate yet."

December began with a morale boosting 5-2 shellacking of Everton in the Merseyside derby. Mohamed Salah, Roberto Firmino and Jordan Henderson were all consigned to the bench and Alisson Becker sat it out through suspension. Eyebrows were raised when fringe players like Dejan Lovren, Xherdan Shaqiri and Divock Origi were brought into the fold but a rampant Reds put their visitors to the sword.

Bournemouth away and Watford at home brought up another six points for the Reds before Qatar called for the Club World Cup. A return to domestic action arrived on Boxing Day with arguably the performance of the season. Brendan Rodgers's Leicester had to be considered title rivals when the two teams kicked off on December 26, but within 90 minutes, those claims were considered laughable as a ruthless Reds left town with a convincing 4-0 triumph. Merry Christmas indeed.

Alexander-Arnold couldn't suppress a laugh as he learned of his 10 in the ECHO's player ratings as Virgil van Dijk urged his team-mates not to let up as the title started to emerge on the horizon. "We have to keep it going," he said from the bowels of the King Power. The Reds were refusing to deviate from the script. To a man, Liverpool were on-message.

After Wolves had again rattled City the following day, Liverpool's lead stood at a daunting 13 points. To virtually everyone outside the Anfield bubble, the title was decided before the Christmas lights had been turned off.

A quick-fire pair of wins at home against Wolves and Sheffield United added half-a-dozen more points to the pot. Energy levels understandably dipped, but the results remained the same. Klopp's team were cruising towards the title. A first visit to the Tottenham Hotspur Stadium was a successful one as Roberto Firmino's goal settled it in favour of the away side in London in January.

By now, a 16-point advantage was opened up. Liverpool had set a record for the best-ever start to a season in any of Europe's top-five leagues but Klopp was refusing to get carried away. "When someone gives you a trophy it is done but until then you need to fight," he said as he fielded questions, post-match. "It is only the start. We need to continue because our contenders are so strong."

"We don't ever want to be complacent," Adam Lallana said. "And it's good to look back and see places you can improve. That's a good mentality to have."

Eight days later, even The Kop started to believe this was their year.

As Mohamed Salah streaked clear of Daniel James to make it 2-0 against Manchester United, the Anfield faithful tried out a new terrace anthem as he ripped off his shirt in jubilation. "And you're gonna believe us...we're gonna win the league!"

Salah lost his kit, the Kop lost its mind, Man City lost the league. Alisson Becker was first to arrive on the scene as a shirtless Salah was smothered by team-mates. Anfield erupted. Game over.

It was a symbolic moment of release that saw Liverpool finally anoint themselves as the next champions of England long after everyone else had done so.

The Reds fans had proudly boasted about being top of the table all season, but there was a tangible shift on January 19. Now, they felt, with much conviction, that the Premier League crown would finally be theirs. A special home in the Anfield cabinet awaited the first trophy of its kind.

And yet still, Klopp was unwilling to indulge. For him, that was the job of others. Those who had paid their hard-earned to witness history unfold.

"Of course they are allowed to dream and sing whatever they want, and as long as they do their job in the moment we play, all fine," he said. "But we will not be part of that party yet."

Yet.

Sixteen points became 22 when the Reds followed up a win at West Ham with a 4-0 drubbing of Southampton at the beginning of February before Klopp claimed: "We're not even close to being perfect."

The serenity was pierced by a sharp defeat at Watford at the end of that month however, as Liverpool's hopes of invincibility fell by the wayside in Hertfordshire after one of the worst Reds performances in years.

It was nothing but a minor hiccup, but the ever-increasing threat of the coronavirus continued to course its way across the globe. Less than two weeks later, play would be suspended.

With just six more points needed after a return to winning ways at home to Bournemouth, Liverpool were made to shelve their plans for glory. A waiting game ensued.

Football was given its return date in May. June 21 would see Liverpool travel to Everton for the 236th Merseyside derby, behind closed doors. The surreal prospect of winning a first league title in 30 years at Goodison Park without a fan in attendance was briefly on the agenda depending on the result of City's visit from Arsenal.

By now, even Klopp was willing to let his guard down, openly discussing the prospect of bus parades to mark the moment.

"If this is the 12th or 13th matchday of next season and we want to celebrate it - who is going to stop it?" said the Liverpool boss. "Then we still have the trophy and then we can drive it around town and stand on the bus. If other people then think that we are completely crazy, I honestly don't care."

A bore draw was quickly forgotten about at Goodison Park after the relentless chasing of Crystal Palace left the visitors in a daze as Anfield played host to its first match since mid-March.

A 4-0 victory would get the job done for the Reds. Twenty-four hours later, they had their collective feet up in Formby Hall as Chelsea beat City to confirm what we had all known for a long time.

Liverpool were the best team in the land. As Klopp said, Anfield is a place for big football moments.

You'll Never Walk Alone

It is little wonder that people talk about having goosebumps when they hear this. It is different to similar experiences at other clubs because YNWA is universally famous.

It is a shared emotional experience at group level - as a group collective. This shared experience heightens the sense of collective identity. It is a hymn of community - a war cry of determination verging on invincibility.

YNWA and to a degree the colour Red become an expression of identity, of belonging, of meaning. YNWA is an emotional experience tied to memory and meaning. It galvanises belief and fighting spirit.

It galvanises the crowd who then will the players on and the 'Twelfth Man' is very real. The Twelfth Man drives the players on.

The belief and fighting spirit of the collective is embodied by Klopp as an individual. Liverpool play in waves and eventually waves will erode any rock.

Klopp's style tactically and as an individual on the touchline play to the strengths of the Twelfth Man. Nothing is impossible. The fans are not passive.

During lockdown the Twelfth Man was missing and the club and certain players recognised this and made a big effort to engage fans. Milner and Robertson for instance were very active on Twitter - this was them reaching out to the fans. Wanting to maintain the connection.

In an empty stadium players are feeding on their own resources. I have watched games from inside the empty stadium. There is almost an eeriness. But an atmosphere WAS created.

And the atmosphere that Liverpool manage to create inside an empty stadium owes much to Klopp who is undoubtedly inspirational - a supreme motivator.

Dr Gillian Cook

You'll Never Walk Alone

YNWA is more than a song, it's a mantra, a lifestyle.

Been over a few times in recent years and met loads of great Reds through Twitter that have become more than just a name on a computer screen.

Nigel Coady, New Ross

When you walk into Anfield the electric atmosphere pings all around the ground through the supporters to the players.
You get nothing like this at any other club. You'll Never Walk Alone gives you goosebumps no matter how many times you hear it. It never fails to get you hyped.

Macaulay Stone, Kidderminster

The first game I ever tuned into was during the 18/19 season. I heard You'll Never Walk Alone sung for the first time and became a Red.

John Cooper, Lebanon, Pennsylvania, USA

If there was a song to unite the world, then this is the song. We are all different but when we sing the song, we are one.

Jacob Chacko, Singapore

YNWA is a really good life motto to live by.

Joshua Engelbrecht, Durban, South Africa

Madness

Football turns normal, sensible, intelligent people into irrational maniacs. It makes us do things we don't want to do and behave in ways we can't explain and aren't proud of. I kiss the dog when Newcastle score. I thought I was mad. I wasn't even close....

Alastair Machray

Madness

It was immense, the whole season. I was working the day we beat Aston Villa away, with the two late goals. I work in a bookies'. When Robbo scored the equaliser, I celebrated, spun around, and punched one of our customers (unintentionally). He was fine, but was gone before Sadio scored the winner.

Nigel Coady, New Ross

I held hands with my mate and refused to let go after the Jerzy Dudek save in 05. I was convinced that if I let his hand go we would lose the game. I didn't and we didn't. So maybe I was right.

Ian Byrne, Accra, Ghana

I named my son Ryan..... after Ryan Babel, my favourite former Liverpool FC player

Kelvin Osiro, Nairobi

When we won European Cup in 2005 I was in a pub with my friends. When we won I jumped up and my head went through the plaster ceiling - luckily the owner was ok and saw funny side.

Tony Lockey, Hawick

When we won in Istanbul I ran up and down the street in my boxer shorts (not a pretty sight).

Matt Green, Birmingham

The whole season I dodged work and gave excuses every weekend because I wanted not to miss matches. I got sacked. In Uganda we try to find jobs for everyone. If you're a Liverpool fan with a truck you come first.

Steven Mukopya, Kampala, Uganda

Last season I got to the point where I physically couldn't watch any games as the nerves destroyed the enjoyment. I kept expecting us to slip up. When we went into Lockdown someone asked me how I was feeling, to which I replied: 'I can't believe we're going to lose this title after being 25 points clear.' 'No!', they said, 'I mean about your daughter's wedding not going ahead.'

Steve Livingston, Barrow-in-Furness

You don't go out on a Saturday night if the result is bad. I've ended relationships because the girls didn't understand why.

Anthony Crosbie, Dublin, Ireland

I wrote an email while still intoxicated to John Henry and his wife Linda. I invited them to my humble abode for a cup of tea or a beer so I could thank them for looking after my beloved club I said if they were in the area feel free to pop in…

John Dempsey, Kirkby

A colleague brought me a Barcelona scarf back from a trip a few years ago because he knows I like football. I'm not a Barca fan. When LFC beat Barca I ran outside with the Barca scarf and stomped on it in front of my house.

Ellen Zierk, Beverley, Massachusetts, USA

I remember when we overturned the result against Barcelona at Anfield. It was an unbelievable moment that will forever be in my memory.

Egbeyinka Moses, Lagos State, Nigeria

I injured my friend because he was trying to insult LFC.

Kelechi Chukwu, Nigeria

People in Mbale City call me LIVERPOOL instead of my real name.

Basil Wanzira, Mbale, Uganda

I farted on a United fan when we beat them at Old Trafford.

Emmanuel Yalley, Takoradi, Ghana

21

I once said I had the 'flu and couldn't go to work so I could go to Derby away. I was spotted on the telly in the front row with my distinctive ski jacket on. And one of the lads from work was also on our coach. I was 'let go' a couple of weeks later.

Roy Gates, Wallasey

I won a prize on a radio sports programme. When I went to get it, it turned out to be a Man Utd calendar signed by Rooney and co. I refused to accept it and told the presenter how shit he made me feel.

Yahaya Murana, Lagos, Nigeria

I once sat in an airport for three hours with a towel over my head, avoiding speaking to anybody to avoid hearing a result.

Rob Greene, Oswestry

I downloaded videos and photos of the Liverpool team lifting the trophy. I was so happy I slaughtered a hen in jubilation.

David Ssewante, Uganda

When we won five trophies in 2001 under Houllier I walked into my Man Utd-supporting boss's office and put a football boot on his desk. I told him to give it to his Man Utd players so that they could learn how to play football.

Richard Monneron, Mauritius

I was born a Red and will die one. Dad was from Birkenhead. Grandad told me I was never to marry a Manc.

Jacquie Adlington, Chesterfield

Years ago I barred a girlfriend from the house. We were playing Bayer Leverkusen in 2002 and every time she walked into my bedroom we conceded a goal. After the third time it happened I told her to leave the house. We split up soon after.

Gavin Conlan, Essex

When Neil Mellor scored against Arsenal in 2004 I jumped up, hit my head on a beam and knocked myself unconscious for several minutes.

Okcan Basat, Istanbul, Turkey

Liverpool's playing style has helped my business and improved much on my earnings. The style makes me smile as we play and as we win games. I thus react politely to my customers and hence achieve more of them.

Katsigazi Gaspari, Kampala, Uganda

I couldn't get a ticket for my son for the Barcelona game so ended up going alone. After the match as I was leaving the stadium, my wife sent me a video of him celebrating. It just made me sit down and cry. A big, baldy, 40-year-old man just sitting down, sobbing and laughing at the same time.

David Hughes, Liverpool

I never miss a game for anything and everyone knows not to call me or text me when we play because I won't respond. And don't even think about inviting me anywhere when we play, because I won't be there. My wife is a bit jealous. A few years ago we were playing midweek and I had the TV on full blast and was standing in front of it (I always watch matches standing up). She said: 'Why are Liverpool playing now? I thought they only play weekends?' I told her midweek was Champions League. She said: 'Ooohh I fuckin' hate Liverpool. I wish they'd just break up.' I told that story at my wedding. Everyone was crying with laughter.

Colin Finn, Ballaghaderreen, Co Roscommon, Ireland

Drove to the Cup Final ticketless. Blew my mini's engine up and had to leave it on the M1 and hitchhike to Wembley. Managed to bunk in and saw us lose. Had to pay £300 to fix my mini's engine when we got it back from the bizzies.

Alyn Janes, Denmark

On numerous occasions I broke South Africa's Lockdown rules to watch LFC at friends' houses. I bought booze on the black market, had a jolly good time and broke curfew on the way home.

Gordon Upton, Port Elizabeth, South Africa

I can't really put into words just how much the club means to me. The only thing I love more is the wife but don't tell her I said that.

Kev Nelson, Prenton, Merseyside

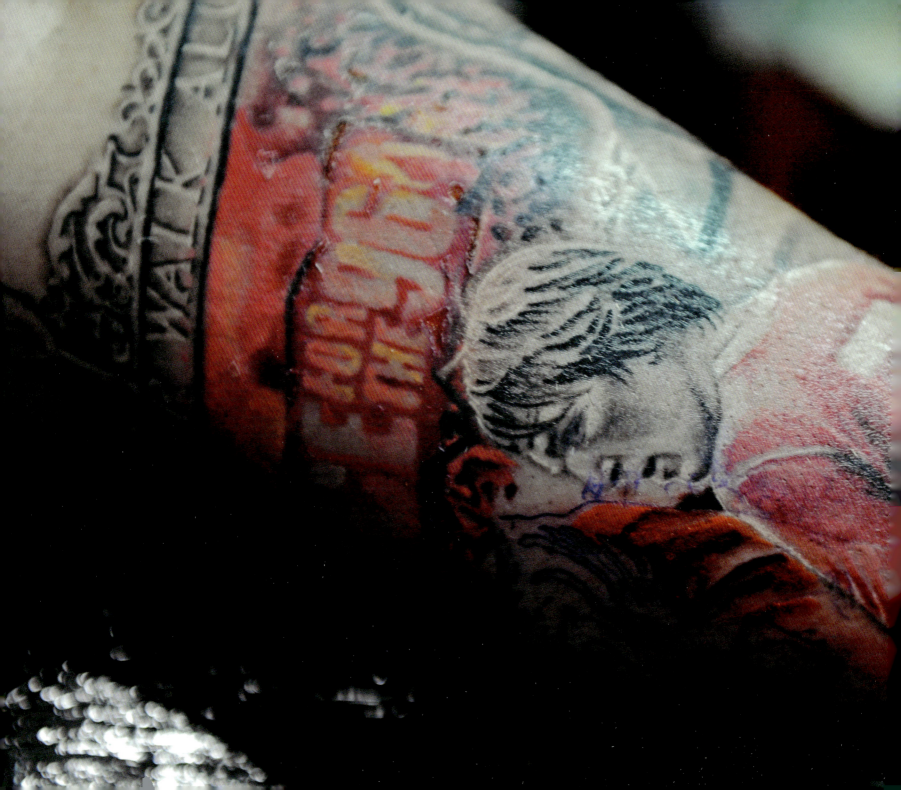

A Special bond

Covid had a big impact on everyone. The research discovers a similar situation in other worldwide pandemics of the past too. It creates issues of anxiety, boredom, depression, loneliness - all present during Lockdown. On top of that came the uncertainty over the League. What would happen if the League was declared void? Would we be robbed?

The government recognised that they needed to alleviate loneliness, boredom and isolation and football was one of the ways they saw of doing this. That's why they wanted football to have a comeback, They saw it as providing hope, and also as a galvanising effect.

Dr Gillian Gook

A Special bond

No other club could turn over a 3-0 deficit against the great Barcelona or pull off the stunning comeback against Olympiakos. The fans make the impossible possible and that is why we are able to make history and achieve so much. The opposition is intimidated by Anfield. God help them if they go behind within 10 minutes.

Macaulay Stone, Kidderminster

It's to do with the scouse diaspora. I live in London but my mum's from Huyton and my dad's from Parliament St. The Scouse way is inclusive - it is a mix of Irish, Welsh, Chinese, Caribbean, in fact cultures from all over the world. And there's a working-class unity too.

John Owen Salkeld, London

The passion we hold for the club is massive and there is only one group of supporters who can impact a game in the way Liverpool fans can. Just look at the Barca game, that wouldn't have happened if it wasn't for the fans. Nowhere else in sport will you find that passion and impact.

Tobias Nilsson-Gjörloff, Växjö, Sweden

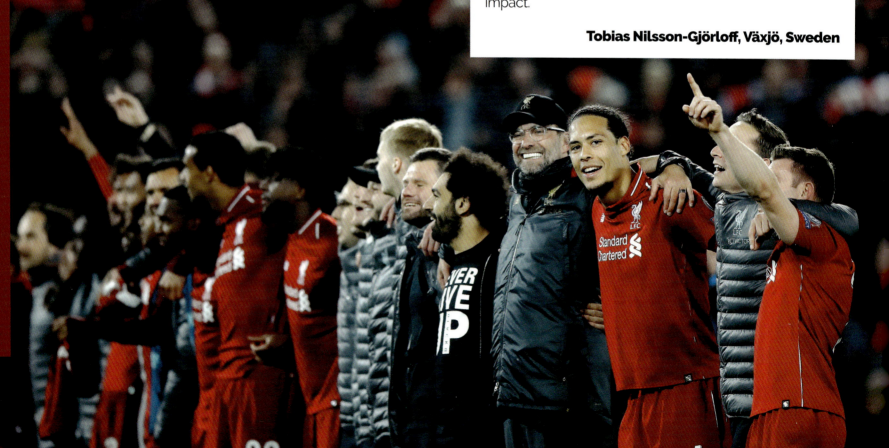

When the team is in times of struggle that's when our fans show their class. It is no coincidence that we have had so many comebacks - there are no white hankies or booing. The struggle makes us louder and our support stronger.

Norman Jones, Holyhead, North Wales

When we formed the Melbourne Overseas Liverpool Supporters Club back in 2005 I saw 500-plus jam-pack a pub in Melbourne to watch Istanbul. You realise just how strong the ties are. We're a true global family. I don't say that half baked either. It doesn't matter where you go if you see a fellow Red you immediately have a friend for life. YNWA is not just a song. It's a way of life for us.

Wayne Psalia, Adelaide Australia

I carry with me the LFC 'never-say-never' attitude. There is always light at the end of every storm. I walk on with my head held up high, always.

Simbarashe Farirepi, Harare, Zimbabwe

Whilst the other successful English teams' fans are consumed by hate towards LFC I feel that we do not harbour that same resentment and vile hostility. We support our team and that's it.

Keiron Delaney, Newport, South Wales

I was diagnosed with Parkinson's in 2008. My life changed for the worse. But without my memories and being able to stand on the Kop and sing my lungs out, I would be lost. Just being there helps me belong and blots out this bloody disease. At the end of a storm.

John Dempsey, Kirkby

Liverpool fans feel more like a community. Once you choose this team, it's a lifetime commitment. LFC fans support their team through highs and lows.

Ellen Zierk, Beverley, Massachusetts, USA

I have supported them all my life. I shook hands with Bill Shankly and Bob Paisley.

Bernie Howden, Wirral

Caught a coach up from Bournemouth for the 1978 Super Cup clash with Anderlecht and went to Sir Kenny Dalglish's house the night before to wish him all the best. He answered the door in his slippers and was very understanding and friendly to two lads from the south coast - miles from home. What a legend!

Steven Ives, Sandbanks, Dorset

We had just been knocked out of the European Cup by Nottingham Forest which meant we could not win it three times on the bounce. Everyone just started singing YNWA. That was belief. It's not blind faith it's just belief. Belief that next time we will still be together - fans and team. It's just ace.

Ian Leatherbarrow, Bromley

The city of Liverpool has been mistreated by the rest of the country in many ways over the last few decades. It's a culturally rich city, deeply misunderstood by many. The club is a massive extension of that. The club and the people have suffered and healed together in ways few other clubs have.

James Bartlett, Ciudad Quesada, Spain

LFC has taken me to places I wouldn't otherwise have been, allowed me to meet people I wouldn't otherwise have met. They are the one true constant and anchor throughout my life, from childhood into adulthood. They allow me, for a few hours a week, to forget everything else and live the moment.

James Haw, Liverpool L25

I've never met a Liverpool fan I didn't like. It's like making an instant brother or sister.

David Coffey, London

Luis Garcia scored the winner against Chelsea in the 2005 Champions League semi-final. It was the fans who scored that goal.

Kibira Geofrey, Uganda

It genuinely feels like the closest thing to a religion that I could relate to. Built on hope, belief and being there for each other in times of need. You don't see that anywhere else.

David Hughes, Liverpool

It's all about being together as one team, the club, the players and the supporters. We are a family.

Paul Scerri, Malta

I think Liverpool fans are more outwardly political than other fans generally. That togetherness and sense of community is something Jürgen Klopp marries perfectly with.

Simon Williams, Peterborough

For me, the Holy Trinity is the fans, the players and the staff. That bond has always been pivotal.

Roy Heaney, Crosby, Merseyside

Liverpool is not a 'fanbase' it's a family. Nowhere else in the world could you celebrate a last-minute winner with an old fella, hug him and share your emotions with him... then never see him again after that moment.

Jay O'Brien, Kirkby, Merseyside

We are special, because of what we have seen. We are special because we come from diverse backgrounds. We are special because we embrace difference. What defines us is our never-say-die attitude, the fight in our hearts, the struggle to prove people wrong. Justice for the 96.

Ian Byrne, Accra, Ghana

My first trip to Liverpool was amazing. I had been to see Liverpool play matches in London around the turn of the century but didn't make my first pilgrimage to Anfield until 2014. I was instantly made to feel welcome by strangers who seemed to appreciate that I'd taken the time to come over and support the Reds in person.

Kevin Ryan, Orlando, Florida, USA

In the 80s I broke my leg. I went on The Kop on crutches every week, and hopped down the central walkway between the two uprights holding the roof up. The crowd opened up: 'Here comes Peg Leg, make way for Peg Leg' and a sea of fans parted, making space for me to get my spec. I felt well protected, looked after and they even went and got me a tea at half time. It only came with sugar in those days as it all got poured into one great big urn.

Kevin Wallace, Windsor

It becomes the centre of everything I do; how I plan my life both short term and long term, how I plan weekends and activities. It plays a huge part in my mood for the week and gives me structure and distraction.

Kjel Van Rossem, Putte, Belgium

I have had numerous medical issues and major spinal surgery. What kept me going was the LFC culture of never giving up; the spirit of Shankly; the way the boys keep playing until the end. It makes me believe that no matter how many times my problems knock me down, I will get back up and carry on fighting.

Mary Urbanowski, Walton, Liverpool

Rituals

Superstitions and rituals can help to bring a sense of control and predictability.

Rituals are a perfect example of fans refusing to be passive. It is not surprising Liverpool fans take refuge in rituals. This is them saying: 'We are helping to influence' rather than simply observing and hoping.

Dr Gillian Cook

Rituals

I always sit in the same spot whenever the match is on.

Ajit Alexander, Dubai

Me and my mum drive along the river singing You'll Never Walk Alone, Allez Allez Allez and Virgil Van Dijk's song (it has to be in that order). I wear my TAA shirt with my AOC shirt around my neck. I have my Lucky Candle which I have to keep buying.

Ellie Humphries, Aigburth

Since my Grandad passed away in 2018 I take his old bus pass with me in my top pocket. I also kick the seat in front of me four times, twice with each foot. I also do the cross sign and ask my Grandad to help us win.

Marc Williams, Melling Mount, Merseyside

Always wear my lucky scarf; NEVER say the name of the opposition. Always watch with my son and daughters each match. Kiss the dog when we win.

Tony Lockey, Hawick

I bake. The tension always gets to me so I usually bake for most of the matches. My son sets his Liverpool cushion in the lounge on the sofa for Premier League matches, and his scarf in front of the TV for Champions League matches. While he was at university, he would text me to make sure I did it for him at home.

Rintha Ranjit, Port Shepstone, South Africa

Meet in the Anfield Cafe before home games and always have a small breakfast and a cup of tea, whatever the day, time or weather.

Mark Dixon, Croston

I silently pray before watching every LFC game, even if it's a repeat and I know the score.

Sam-Abel Gbinsay, Monrovia, Liberia

I talk to Shanks in every game asking him for help from above.

Paul Burke, Arklow, Co Wicklow, Ireland

I always hang up my Liverbird flag for big matches and I always take my 1974 No 7 away shirt on holiday. And I NEVER miss an opportunity to wind up ManUre fans (although the 90s were very tough).

Steven Ives, Sandbanks, Dorset

On the way to winning the league every time I had a drink I had to stir it ten times. Then we won it so I don't have to.

Graham King, Birmingham

I sit in my miniature LFC changing room before games with YNWA playing through the speakers.

Joacim Niaminem, Nynashamn, Sweden

I always watch the game from the same seat in my mancave named Anfield.

Ree Van Heerden, East London, South Africa

We all wear our newest Liverpool shirts and scarves sitting at home watching the match. We are the Twelfth Man.

Andrew Jones, Liverpool

I always wear red undies on matchdays.

Jacquie Adlington, Chesterfield

I have little figures of Jürgen and Mo Salah that I place in front of the TV.

Stephen Taylor, Surrey, British Columbia, Canada

Matchday I have my lucky LFC shirt, with my lucky black hoodie, my lucky pants and socks, and my lucky green coat for the winter games. I have to put my wristbands on in a certain order followed by my watch. Before each match me and my mates have to take our lucky pre-match team photo and it has to be shared in our WhatsApp group for others that aren't at the match.

Gavin Conlan, Essex

In the 80s I'd go to the chippy on Breck Road and buy sausage and chips then go onto the Kop early and read the matchday programme.

Rob Cowan, Brighton

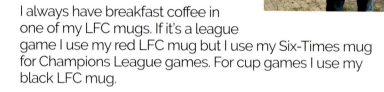

I always have breakfast coffee in one of my LFC mugs. If it's a league game I use my red LFC mug but I use my Six-Times mug for Champions League games. For cup games I use my black LFC mug.

Peter Locke, Isle of Man

I wear my Liverpool shirt my grandchildren bought me. It says NANA on the back.

Bridget McDonald, Knowsley

I do the Benitez ritual every Liverpool home game - I sit with my legs crossed.

Emmanuel Yalley, Takoradi, Ghana

I always watch in full kit and with scarves on the telly. When Liverpool have a set piece to defend I have to whisper the same phrase over and over with my hands over my mouth.

Kjel Van Rossem, Putte, Belgium

Guinness before the game. Same turnstile, same toilet cubicle (will even wait for it). One time I was wearing new earrings and we were getting beat. So I took them off. And we won. Yes, I'm mad.

Su Wilson, Runcorn

I have a specific mug I drink my coffee out of when I watch matches. It's not even an LFC mug, it's a Star Wars mug. I drank out of it when we beat City 4-3 to end their unbeaten run in 2017-18 and I just kept doing it.

Sean Whooley, Boston, USA

Our lot used to take a tin of tuna to matches, it brought us luck! The bigger the tin, the better the result.

Kevin Wallace, Windsor

On match days I park up at my uncle's house off Breck Road and have a burger at the same stall before the game. My son has to have curry and chips after.

Paul Carine, Tadcaster, North Yorkshire

When we go the game, we always go the fan park in Anfield Road and my boy plays football in the little football set-up. We did it two years ago when he went to his first game and we do it every time now.

David Hughes, Liverpool

Lucky socks, lucky undies, lucky scarf. I wear a tee shirt dedicated to my Brother Billy. I visit his memorial stone on 96 Avenue before each home match.

Ian Sword, Birkenhead

We sing, we wear our shirts and hang our flags out. And have a big hotdog.

Alfie Baker, aged 7, Lydiate, Merseyside

If we are playing at home I always make sure that the volume on the radio or the TV has the first number greater than the last. This stems from the fact that the home team score is stated before the away. E.g 40 in volume means 4-0 to us that coming evening. If we are playing away, the volume might be 39, so you get the picture. We haven't won an away game 9-3 in my lifetime. But I still persist with it.

Soumen Saha, Bromley

COLIN LANE
The Liverpool Echo's veteran Chief Photographer
shares his season through a lens

The Moment of Triumph

For me the 2019-20 title won't be damaged or carry any negativity at all. This is because the full League has been played. It wasn't a case of deciding the league on average points per game or anything like that as it was in some other leagues. Had they done this it would have been tainted but they didn't, they completed the full programme of fixtures,

And I actually think it will be more memorable. In ten years' time people will ask who won the 2019-2020 Premier League? And it will be more memorable, more special, because people will remember the season for Coronavirus. Yet if you ask in 10 years who won in 2017-18 for instance, will people know? Or will they say: Was it Man City? Or was it Chelsea? Liverpool's victory will always be remembered.

Dr Gillian Cook

The Moment of Triumph

I felt justice. And pride. Times a million.

Andy O'Neill, Huyon

There was overwhelming happiness and relief. Then there was seeing my daughter's face knowing it was the first time she had seen them win it, Then I saw King Kenny - and that reduced this middle-aged man to tears.

Norman Jones, Holyhead, North Wales.

A bottle of beer from Homegrown Collective and a FaceTime chat with my best friend Laura.

Gary Bradburn, Huyton

I slaughtered a goat and we enjoyed with my teammates.

Mubiru Farouque, Nsangi Kampala, Uganda

I was home celebrating and wishing that, as a member of the Official Supporters Club of New York, I would have loved to have been at our home at the 11th Street Bar. I cracked open a bottle of champagne and enjoyed a glass or two of that with my wife. Was up all night celebrating with friends on the phone, texting, zooming and FaceTiming with people all over the world.

Tim Mahoney, New Jersey, USA

Relief. Overwhelming relief. I've spent most of my working life in Manchester watching them slowly claw at our records, being ripped by colleagues and mates who honestly thought Liverpool FC would never come back. Seeing us go close on a handful of occasions was excruciating. Then the moment came, at the blow of a whistle we were back at the top.

Ian Byrne, Accra, Ghana

The joy when we won the league was the best I have experienced. Before that it was a rollercoaster. I was nervous we may slip up to Man City then, when Covid-19 kicked in, I was worried the league would be void.

Stuart Beattie, Lochmaben, Scotland

I have a long standing battle with my brothers who are Man Utd fans. I played You'll Never Walk Alone the whole night so they couldn't sleep.

Stuart Kyazze, Kigali, Rwanda

It was one of those rare moments where tears and goosebumps collide. In a good way.

Pierina Chang, Johor Bahru, Malaysia

I went to bed and slept well for the first time since Lockdown. No one could take it off us now. Lockdown was like the longest VAR referral on Earth.

David Coffey, London

It was uncontrolled. I killed one big goat for people to celebrate with me for almost eight hours.

Chukwuma Shedrach, Ozalla, Nigeria

We got in the car, flags flying, drove to a mate's house and had a party in his front garden, draining his car battery playing and singing Liverpool songs before walking home to a chorus of car horns.

James Haw, Liverpool L25

I was crying. I wanted to scream so the whole world could hear me. I wanted to go onto the balcony and scream "We fucking won the league" It was the first time in my lifetime.

Dare Adebayo, Ogun State, Nigeria

The tears came streaming down my cheeks. I called my father in Ireland to share the moment with him but after 30 years of struggle I was unable to talk. It was amazing to have finally done it, but the memories of all the close times came flooding back. Now it was real. We had done it, and those who I most wanted to share the moment with were on the other side of the Atlantic.

Morgan O'Sullivan, Boynton Beach, Florida

It was 2:30 am and I was with my brother. I couldn't shout or scream as my parents were asleep. I took that emotion to Instagram and, in a video, just blurted out everything I felt. I don't regret posting a single thing.

Kavinka Fernando, Colombo, Sri Lanka

I remembered a conversation I'd had with a friend who brought up the fact that I was in my 70s. I told him I'd had a great life but I wanted Liverpool to win the Premier League before I met my maker. In the 60s, 70s, 80s I would have got blind drunk. I'm 73 now so I just got merry.

Ken Parry, Carnforth

It felt like something had been missing and I had found it. It felt like completion.

Alexis Syleks, Paris

I was so happy and proud for the boys. To have such a crazy season happen and have them win and celebrate all together at a hotel was so beautiful. It was the first true joy I felt in a post-Covid world.

Kate Keefe, Lowell, Massachusetts, USA

I cried my eyes out while holding my sister's picture (she died four years ago) and telling her we were back to where we belong. I hope she sees and knows how brilliant that season was.

Vicki Parry, Shrewsbury

I got drunk and bought a load of Liverpool stuff online. Got the Echo souvenir paper too. I'm gonna get it framed. Got a replica medal too. I also put a Liverpool flag on the Iron Man statue on the motorway near my house linking the West of Ireland to Dublin. I put a pic on social media and the dirty Mancs took down the flag that night. I put another flag up, with 'Never Give Up' written on it. Didn't put it on social media. It lasted five weeks this time, but the dirty Mancs took it down again. I have another flag that I'm going to put on with steel cable ties so they won't be able to take it down so handy

Colin Finn, Ballaghaderreen, Co Roscommon, Ireland

My best mate Joe and his girlfriend Rach came around and we stood on the step (socially distanced) having a beer and watched as the fireworks went off all over the city. I get goosebumps still thinking of that night.

Kyle Serrao, Orrell Park, Liverpool

The People who matter

At times of intense emotion we want to be with people who are closest to us - people with whom we have created shared memories. It is natural that our first thoughts at times of intense emotion are for family members.

Dr Gillian Cook

The People who matter

I was stranded in Ghana due to Covid-19. My wife and family had been evacuated back to the UK in March. So it was the first trophy in my 10-year-old son's life and we weren't together to see the Hendo shuffle. I watched the trophy-lift with a mate, an Arsenal fan - who was made up for us. Even if he did keep harping on about Michael Thomas.

Ian Byrne, Accra, Ghana

I missed having my uncle with me as he "sold" LFC to me as a four-year-old kid

Pravesh Dursan, Durban, South Africa

I had flashbacks of all of the games that I have been to and my first game at the age of 7. Flashbacks of all the greats to have played for Liverpool and flashbacks of the ups and downs along this emotional rollercoaster. When they stopped I could only think of my beloved mother who passed away five years ago and who couldn't be with us to see us crowned champions. We brought her ashes back to Allerton Cemetery.

Stuart Wilson, Johannesburg, South Africa

As the clock ticked down, I thought of my Dad, who died in August 2018. The emotions of that, and the 30-year wait, came flooding out. Happy tears though.

Gary Bradburn, Huyton

We lost my uncle in October 2019 as the possibility of us finally winning the league became more real. We then lost my Dad in February of this year just before Covid-19. The emotion of these losses coupled with the very real prospect of the league being voided meant that 'difficult time' didn't even scratch the surface. When we were eventually confirmed champions I cried tears of joy - but there was also immense sadness that my two best friends never got to see us lift the trophy.

Colin Murray, Port Talbot

We ate, drank, sang. We were socially distancing from others although my husband, son, grandson and nephew who live at our home are frontline workers. We decided to stay at home but we decorated the whole house outside.

Jane King, Kirkby, Merseyside

All my life has been about Liverpool FC and it reminds me of my dad. The match makes me seem closer to him and my grandad. Now my boys go to Anfield it means four generations of us have stood on the Kop.

Graham King, Birmingham

My thoughts went to my friend that passed the previous year even though he was a staunch fan of that lot up in Old Trafford. The abuse and banter I would have given him would have been ferocious

Anthony Crosbie, Dublin, Ireland

I was with my son who's a Man Utd fan. I just wished my brother who is a huge fan of Liverpool had been alive to see us win it. He died tragically in February 2020.

**Latoyia Hinds-Brown,
St Catherine, Jamaica**

I cried for Steven Gerrard because he worked so hard for Liverpool but he didn't lift the Premier League.

Kiberua Moses, Kampala, Uganda

I wished my mum, an LFC angel, could have been with me to celebrate.

Tina Diaper, Southampton

I was on my own and thoughts went immediately to my best friend Dave who was by my side on our many journeys following the Reds. He sadly passed away in January 2020. At full time I punched the heavens and said: 'Cheers Dave, we've finally done it.'

Graham Neaves, Cyprus

I was very excited when Jordan Henderson finally lifted the trophy...it was even more satisfying because my African brothers played important roles in pushing LFC on to breaking the three-decade curse.

Gyamfi Compassion Karikari, Accra, Ghana

I missed my sister. She had Down's Syndrome and passed away at the age of 44. She used to phone me after every match as she loved Liverpool FC so much - especially Stevie G. I used to buy her lots of Liverpool things.

Joseph, Attard, Malta

I missed those people that I've travelled the country and the continent with, the people I've shared car journeys, flights, many a pint with, years, laughter and too many matches to count.

James Haw, Liverpool L25

One of our away day mates, Grousey, designated driver for the 2004/05 campaign, sadly passed away during the pandemic. We would have given him a big LFC send off but we've not been able to unfortunately, but we will do! Thought of my Dad, and of Grousey, and had a feeling of them looking down as we clinched the title.

Dave Whittall, Cheshire

I was alone. I missed all the Manchester United fans who've been making fun of me for the past 15 years.

Stephen Anokye, Ghana

I really missed my matchday travelling lads, Marc and Dan, but most of all my friend Carol who died just before we won the sixth European Cup. She was one of our gang, went everywhere on the European footy trips, up and back to Liverpool for evening matches, getting home at 4am. The massive packed lunches she would make for us in the car! Enough for 10 people and only four of us in it! She was desperate to see us win the Premiership. This one was for her, and all those Reds that have left this world.

Kevin Wallace, Windsor

After my dad passed away in September, I buried him in my 2019-20 home shirt. For the rest of the season, I wore his 2017-18 away shirt for every game. One of the last things he said to me was 'I'll never get to see Liverpool win the league.' So after Chelsea beat Man City, I took a Champions flag to his grave and planted it in the ground. I said: 'We did it. That's for you!'

Richard Fitzsimons, West Derby, Liverpool

My dad passed away from Covid-19 in April 2020. He was hanging on to see us lift the trophy and we had plans to see the game together. I promised him we'd win it and I only hope, wherever he was, he had the biggest celebration and a huge grin on his face.

Steph Littler, Wirral

Why Red?

There is much more to being a football fan than attending matches - it provides a topic of conversation that enables people to relate to each other, Its return provided a re-establishment of identity and commitment. BELONGING.

Belonging is a basic psychological need and a basic driver of human behaviour.

Football gives a sense of family and improves social interaction, It affords a bonding experience between fan and fan, not just between fan and club.

I know when I meet other fans of my club we talk initially about our club then discover other ties and shared interests, It promotes friendship, group cohesiveness and shared emotion, It is a social driver to identify yourself in a group.

Dr Gillian Cook

Why Red?

In the first Liverpool match I watched in the early 80s, I was mesmerised by one player - Kenny Dalglish.

Rintha Ranjit, Port Shepstone, South Africa

In 1974, in school PE class, our gym teacher showed the LFC v Newcastle FA Cup final. I never looked back.

Tony Lockey, Hawick

It sounds like a cliché but our fans are very much a family. Anywhere in the world if I bump into a fellow supporter it feels like meeting a long-lost friend. Through all of the trials and tribulations we have been through, and the accusations that seem to never go away we have always stuck together.

Colin Murray, Port Talbot, South Wales

I love the history of the club. What the club has achieved. The kind of players they bring into the team. How the club treats African players. How the club relates to the supporters. The fans at Anfield. The YNWA song. The colours.

Harry Awuah Bafour, Kumasi, Ghana

Growing up in Australia during the 70s/80s we were starved of live football. The FA Cup was one of the rare live events. Naturally the 1986 final was a big deal as we had our own boy playing. Saw Skippy hit that goal and was hooked.

Wayne Psalia, Adelaide, Australia

Growing up in Liverpool as a kid, the Hillsborough disaster brought a lot of perspective which stuck with me moving forward as a person and as a fan.

Stuart Wilson, Johannesburg, South Africa

The 1977 European Cup win against Borussia Moenchengladbach. The Reds' performance was exquisite.

Yunos Majeed, Western Melbourne, Australia

I first started supporting the Reds in the late 80s. Players like John Barnes, Alan Hansen and Ian Rush made watching football special.

Jonathan Spittle, Boston, Lincs

Seeing the smile on Emlyn Hughes face as he lifted the European Cup in 1977 and the cameras cutting to the fans waving the checked red-and-white flags. And the feeling that no other sport or no other club would ever make me feel this way.

Tim Mahoney, New Jersey, USA

Brought to my first match in Anfield when I was five by my father and the lifelong love affair began then. Being from Dublin I lived very close to Ronnie Whelan and went to the same school So it's in the blood

Anthony Crosbie, Dublin, Ireland

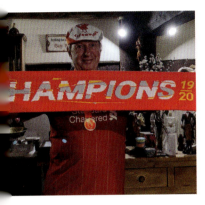

LFC is more than a club - it is a family. My Dad came from Merseyside and the city, the people and the club are very special: caring, humorous, loyal, always willing to help and support. This epitomises everything about LFC.

Ian Kinnear, Great Gate, Staffs

I had tea with Ron Yeats in 1969 and he took me to meet Bill Shankly and the entire squad at the team hotel before a league match with Southampton. I was so excited afterwards that I was sick all night.

Steven Ives, Sandbanks, Dorset

My dad was Irish and told me to support Steve Heighway in the 1971 Cup Final. I'd never seen a game before that as we didn't have a telly. I had no idea what the Cup Final was or where Arsenal and Liverpool were.

David Coffey, London

At my first game the fans were so funny, wise and witty it was like going to the theatre to be entertained.

Peter Archer, Cumbria

I was hooked when my dad took me to my first game on my 6th birthday v Everton and I heard YNWA being sung. Why Red? Just look at the flags. They tell stories.

John Burge, Crosby

I have been able to stand out independently in different areas of my life due to the fact that I'm the only Liverpool fan in my school and I single-handedly banter all other fans.

AbdudHakeem AbdulAzeez, Ekiti State, Nigeria

We are the fairest, funniest and most passionate fans. And not afraid to applaud the opposition.... unless it's the Bitters or Man Utd.

Roy Gates, Wallasey

Because we set the precedent, because we define the narrative, because being different matters, because we appreciate the game as a whole.... Because of our irrational passion and love, which leads us to lose all perspective in the moment, because we are also able to help each other regain that perspective and appreciate what truly matters in the grand scheme.

James Haw, Liverpool L25

LFC just caught my attention more than any other club. Stevie G and Torres made such an exciting duo and LFC played amazing football. I've never looked back.

Aish Batra, India

My dad took me to Anfield in 1958 when I was three years of age. So many memories since then. Through the glory years of Bill Shankly, winning the FA Cup for the first time, and all the Championships and trophies. It has made me so very, very happy.

Eddie Burns, Speke

Liverpool as a club are synonymous with the diversity, community and family spirit of the city itself. I am a leftie from a political standpoint, so this, along with the philosophy of Shanks and now Jürgen suits me down to the ground. Despite being a big club, we are anti-establishment (as well as anti-Tory). Aside from family, LFC is pretty much my first thought of the day and the last before bed.

Soumen Saha, Bromley

I got on a train to Wembley when Liverpool played Everton in the final. I didn't have a ticket but it was just about being there in the atmosphere. Fathers, mothers, sons, daughters, grandchildren.... all walking hand-in-hand, Red or Blue. The proudest day of my life. We showed the world how fans should be on that day.

Jane King, Liverpool

I started supporting them in 2013/14 when the Premier League was shown in the US on NBC. LFC was always a team that my Irish family had supported. My American uncle loved them, and I loved Stevie G. The Red Sox connection also solidified things. Now, I love them for their ethos and because Jürgen projects a humanist approach that is refreshing in sports today.

Kate Keefe, Lowell, Massachusetts, USA

I saw my first match at Anfield on April 27, 1957 v West Ham. A 1-0 win from a Billy Liddell penalty. The noise from the Kop left me in no doubt that I was in the right place. I had fallen in love with the Reds.

Peter Locke, Isle of Man

It all started because I fell in love with Steven Gerrard's long-shot ability in Fifa 03. One thing led to another and I started watching games.

Alexis Syleks, Paris

I went to college in Liverpool in 1965. My digs were in St Domingo Grove, around the corner from Anfield and my landlord was a Red. He said to all the students: 'Right lads, who's coming with me to watch the best team in the world?' And we all went along. Stood on the Kop and it was amazing. Hooked.

Mike Roberts, Faversham, Kent

I remember the whole of Wembley singing 'Merseyside' and knowing Liverpool people were different to anyone else. Over the years as you get older and understand the aftermath of Hillsborough more, you realise just how different we are.

David Hughes, Liverpool

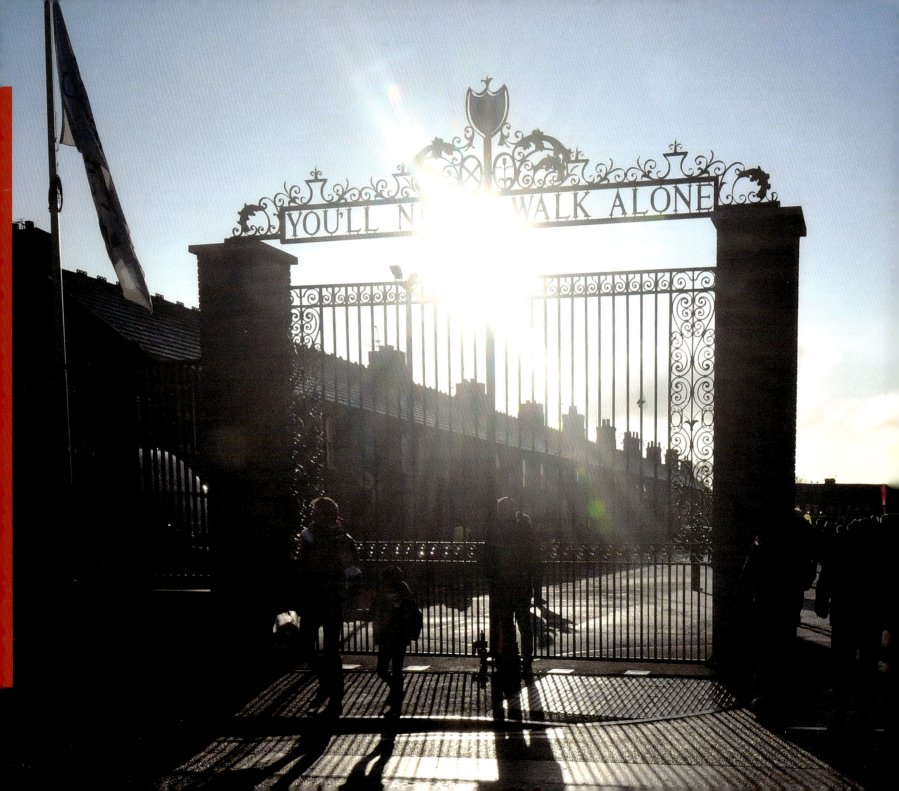

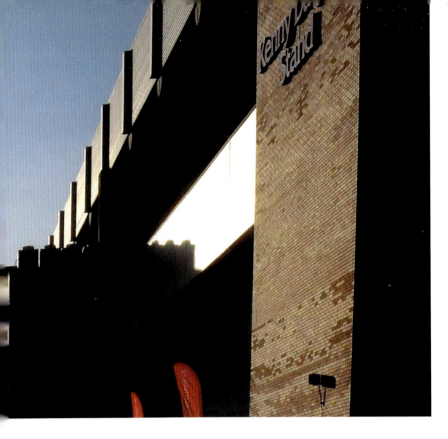

I've been a Red since birth and my love and passion is all consuming. I was lucky enough to sign for the Reds in 1976. Sadly, I broke my leg but went on to have a pro career at Bolton. Football is ingrained in our great city and Liverpool have given me joy in times of heartbreak and hardship. I'm so fortunate to have played at Anfield during my career and remember it as if it was yesterday. Our club transcends football. It's a way of life. It's a love affair. It's draining sometimes but it brings the best out of us and gives us memories we carry for all our lives.

Roy Heaney, Crosby, Merseyside

Originally it was to go against the rest of the family who all supported Everton! I soon realised LFC is more than a club - it's a family engraved on the heart and soul of the city.

Mary Urbanowski, Walton, Liverpool

When I started playing PlayStation with friends most of the other teams were already taken. I had to choose between LFC and Man City. My best friend said: 'Samuel, take LIVERPOOL. They have Steven Gerrard and Fernando Torres. They have Kuyt and Carragher.' So I did and I have never looked back.

Samuel Abasiono, Uyo, Akwa Ibom, Nigeria

They were the nearest team to where I grew up, a half-hour walk away. My aunt took me to my first game in 1979 when I was three years old. I started hanging around the ground for the last 20 minutes in about 1985. By 1988/89, I had my first Kop season ticket.

James Cavanagh, Norris Green, Liverpool

My sister made me a Reds kit for my Teddy bear prior to the 1971 FA Cup final. I was heartbroken that we lost. I've followed the Reds ever since.

Ian Sword, Birkenhead

When I was six or seven, Kevin Keegan played for us and he was an all right player ;). My name was Kevin it went from there.

Kevin Wallace, Windsor

LIVERPOOL ECHO LFC correspondent **PAUL GORST** on Liverpool's legendary 'Twelfth Man' and the agonies and ecstasies of fandom in 2019-2020..

A shirtless Mohamed Salah was tearing around Anfield when the Kop began to stir. As the man so affectionately known as the 'Egyptian King' was picking up the most joyous yellow card of the season for his celebrations, Liverpool fans were finally daring to dream.

After a lifetime of close calls and near falls, this, here and now - against Manchester United, no less - was the moment even these fatigued followers were ready to embrace.

"We're gonna win the league....we're gonna win the league "...And now you're gonna believe us...and now you're gonna believe us "...And now you're gonna believe us...we're gonna win the league!"

Salah lost his shirt. Man United lost the game. The Kop lost its mind.It was a symbolic moment of release that saw Liverpool finally self-anoint themselves as the next champions of England.

A 16-point gap stood between the leaders and Manchester City in second. It was now simply a matter of time before the Premier League's engraver would carve the name 'Liverpool' on to that famous trophy for the first time.

Rewind the clock six months and the Premier League season was just seconds old when the Kop launched into its first hymn of the campaign. It was a boast that hadn't been heard for nearly 15 years on the terraces of Anfield.

"We are the champions...champions of Europe!" came the message as Jürgen Klopp's then-Champions League holders kicked off the new term at home to Norwich on Friday August 9.

A brand new flag was unveiled for the game itself as the patrons recognised Klopp's achievements of June 1 in Madrid by adding his image alongside the greats: Bill Shankly, Bob Paisley, Joe Fagan, Kenny Dalglish and Rafa Benitez.

The message from the Reds fans was clear. Klopp was now viewed alongside the legends for what he had brought back from Spain a few months earlier.

An estimated 750,000 supporters piled onto the city's streets on June 2 to welcome home their heroes as the Liverpool squad proudly paraded the Champions League trophy from atop a bright red bus that crept its way across town during incredible scenes on an unforgettable afternoon.

Klopp's next trick, however, would somehow be even greater.

Between the first game of this history-making season, against Norwich, and the confirmation of Liverpool as Premier League champions in June, the Reds didn't drop a single point at Anfield. Such imperious and impervious home form was not exactly taken for granted, but it was on the road where the fans' memories were truly shaped.

Like when the visiting end marked Roberto Firmino's late winners at Crystal Palace in November or Wolves in January. Or when supporters were handsomely rewarded for their festive loyalty they displayed when trekking to Leicester for an 8pm kick-off on Boxing Day.

These were season-defining moments that were cherished by those who had made the journey. It is what football fandom is built on. The camaraderie, the companionship, the celebration. Liverpool supporters were able to toast to a lifetime of it all.

From a personal perspective, it was a season from the Gods.

Between August and March, as the ECHO's Liverpool FC correspondent, just a few months into the role, I reported on just the one Premier League defeat. Time and again, Klopp's Reds found the will to win, often resulting in hasty re-writes as newspaper deadlines loomed. That, though, was entirely OK by me.

The realisation that I would be the first ECHO correspondent to write about Liverpool winning the league since 1990 had dawned on me a long time before it was confirmed on June 25.

For someone growing up reading and revering the likes of Chris Bascombe, Tony Barrett, Dominic King and my predecessor, James Pearce, that I would be the first reporter at the ECHO for three decades to write those words, was a privilege.

A routine win over Bournemouth at Anfield sent Liverpool 25 points clear. It was now only a matter of time before the winners were confirmed. And then, the darkness. The wilderness.

Football - and its significance - was put firmly into perspective when the action was suspended in mid-March following the outbreak of the coronavirus in the United Kingdom.

For weeks the speculation raged and while the first concern for those inside the Liverpool camp was of the health and safety of the nation, the niggling doubts about what might be the fate of their previous efforts must have lingered. Would their remarkable rise to the cusp of greatness really not be given its reward? It was a very real concern.

For the supporters too, the fans who had travelled the length and breadth of the country in search of the Holy Grail. Fears of a voided Premier League season continued to lurk in the background as anxiety and tension spread across the fanbase.

For good reason too. Opinion was divided over the next course of action and concerns over seeing the campaign called off were almost tangible as Reds followers awaited what was next.

It would be over three months before the action resumed to the sound of silence as the behind-closed-doors model became a necessary evil to kick-start football on these shores once again.

A 4-0 hammering of Crystal Palace on June 24 was a performance deserving of a full house but as the return to Anfield action bore little resemblance to what had gone before it just months earlier, all the Reds could do was keep their end of the bargain.

A month later, the champions would finally get their hands on the trophy they craved above any other. The fireworks burst into the Merseyside sky and Jordan Henderson performed the now-customary 'Hendo Shuffle'. To be one of just 500 in attendance on the night of July 23 is one of the greatest honours of this reporter's lifetime.

As millions of Liverpool fans around the world were forced to huddle around the TV screen for the big moment, the fact I was there to write and report on what was unfolding is something I will never forget.

From doubters, to believers, to achievers. Liverpool supporters must never forget the part they played in it. A generation of dreams came true that night. Mine along with them. The grandkids better get themselves comfortable when it's time for this story to be told.

These are the days.

Biographies

ALASTAIR MACHRAY was editor of the Liverpool Daily Post and Liverpool Echo for 25 years before standing down in 2020 as Britain's longest-serving daily newspaper editor. A lifelong Newcastle United fan, he prides himself on getting as much hate mail from Blues as he does from Reds. He was awarded the MBE in the 2020 Queen's Birthday Honours for Services to Local Journalism.

PAUL GORST is the Liverpool ECHO's LFC correspondent. Joining the ECHO's sports desk in 2016 after previously working for the Daily Mirror, Paul succeeded James Pearce at the beginning of the 2019/20 campaign and reported on every game, home and away, as Jürgen Klopp and his players ended that 30-year wait for a league title. A graduate of the University of Central Lancashire in Preston, Paul has been a sports journalist for over 10 years working for the likes of Mirror Online, the Metro and Goal before joining the ECHO.

DR GILLIAN COOK is a Chartered Sport and Exercise Psychologist. She is a Lecturer in Sport and Exercise Psychology at Liverpool John Moores University. Her research interests include high-performance leadership, and the psychology of performance excellence. She is the first-team and club sport psychologist at Dundee United FC, and has worked with organisations including British Swimming, British Athletics, Scottish Hockey, Loughborough Sport, Nike, the NHS, and BBC. Gillian has been the recipient of various awards including the 2014 British Psychological Society Division of Sport and Exercise Psychology MSc Award for the best MSc dissertation of the year, which was entitled Sport Psychology in an Olympic Swimming Team: Perceptions of the Management and Coaches.